ISBN 978-1-334-23327-2
PIBN 10690803

1 MONTH OF
FREE
READING

at
www.ForgottenBooks.com

By purchasing this book you are eligible for one month membership to ForgottenBooks.com, giving you unlimited access to our entire collection of over 700,000 titles via our web site and mobile apps.

To claim your free month visit: www.forgottenbooks.com/free690803

**English
Français
Deutsche
Italiano
Español
Português**

www.forgottenbooks.com

Mythology Photography **Fiction**
Fishing Christianity **Art** Cooking
Essays Buddhism Freemasonry
Medicine **Biology** Music **Ancient**
Egypt Evolution Carpentry Physics
Dance Geology **Mathematics** Fitness
Shakespeare **Folklore** Yoga Marketing
Confidence Immortality Biographies
Poetry **Psychology** Witchcraft
Electronics Chemistry History **Law**
Accounting **Philosophy** Anthropology
Alchemy Drama Quantum Mechanics
Atheism Sexual Health **Ancient History**
Entrepreneurship Languages Sport
Paleontology Needlework Islam
Metaphysics Investment Archaeology
Parenting Statistics Criminology
Motivational

A Temporary Guide

through the

Engadine Museum

at

St. Moritz

Samaden
Engadine Press Co., formerly Simon Tanner
— 1906 —

A Temporary Guide

Engadine Museum

St. Moritz

Historical notes on the foundation of the Engadine Museum.

F or quite a number of years already the founder and builder of the Museum, Mr. Richard Campell, had been making collection of house-furniture in the characteristic Grison and especially in the Engadine Style. The ardent desire to arrange them all fittingly in sets, and exhibit them to view in an instructive way in suitable rooms, led him on to building for this express purpose a house altogether on old Engadine type, that might be opened to the public as a Museum setting forth the progress of civilisation in some of its aspects in this part of the country.— His architects Messrs. Nicol. Hartmann & Co. encouraging with alacrity this idea of his, he attempted to group, in his mind, a number of rooms in their various wainscotings, with appurtenant corridors, in such a way as might demonstrate to some extent the out-lines of the ground-plan as well as the superstructure of the typical house of the Grisons. The question of location gave rise to great perplexities, since a due regard to a lively frequentation made it desirable to erect the building on none but one of the principal thoroughfares. Yet, the whole scheme would have miscarried, had not Dr. H. Lehmann, Director of the Swiss National Museum in Zurich, who, from the beginning, was well acquainted with this design, and had at all times given it his assistance with his counsels, encouraged the founder to persevere in his project. In the summer of 1905, at last, building commenced and at the beginning of July 1906 the Museum could open its gate.

Structure- and remarkable details
on the Exterior.

The bench in front of the house

The building looks down the valley and shows from top to bottom to great advantage the proportions as well as the simple roofing of a real Engadine house. Steep is the access from the High-road to the great portal, on both sides of which the typical stone-benches covered with boards, invite to rest. Here it is, where, after the daily labours during the short summer months, the household and their neighbours gather to discuss what ever might interest within the narrow mental horizon of a population shut out from the far great world.

The small windows

Corresponding to the needs of the diverse rooms back of them, the small, all but square windows, let deep into the walls, open between oblique faces of the latter like deep-set eyes in a human face, displaying themselves without rule or order all over the façade; yet, they allow by their size and ornaments or their lack of such, of an easy guess at the use, the room behind them is put to: whether they open from the spacious best room (the parlour), to admit without encumbrance of the widest possible outlook into beautiful nature, if this be possible without wasting to much heat from the interior; or whether they are there, merely to give an indispensable amount of light to the kitchen or chamber. For, winter lasts a long time in these high valleys of the Alps, and mercilessly do storms and cold force admittance through even the smallest chinks and cracks. A

The bow

smaller bow-window, facing but in two directions protrudes a little from the façade and affords a view along the high-road in both directions. Here and there, a window is seen as if clothed in projecting lattice-work of really pretty forms. The bow-window, as well as the coat of arms, and the

window trellis

trellis at the window of the corridor on the first floor, were originally on the house of the family of the von Salis in

Celerina, later the house Turtach, very characteristic at the time, but torn down a few years since. They were put on here in the very same old arrangement. Along the outlines of door—and window—frames as well as on the corners of the house, so-called sgraffito-decorations are painted on. **The sgraffitto** They are characteristic of the rhäto-romane house and far **decorations** from causing an effect of plastic substantiality, rather arouse a sensation of plainness even at the corners, which, in themselves, are built so as to give the impression of square pillars. Most of the originals, from which these were copied, are found in Bergün and Filisur.

On the one side of the house facing the Baths is found an imitation of an arbour in the old cloister of Lower- **The arbour of** Schuls; it is rather remarkable for the strict style in the **Lower Schuls** sequence of its vertical development.

The arched Entrance, raised a little above the level of the street, is reached by a short avenue and leads into a wide, vaulted hall built of stone, the so-called Suler. The wooden gate with its baroc ornaments was brought **The gate** from Zernez—and shows an interesting lock of smithing—iron.

A Walk through the Museum.

The Suler occupies the central position among all the **Room I Suler** rooms of the peasant's home in rhäto-romane parts. It is called into service as a store-room, as a working-room for divers house-work and cultivator's doings, for dances and games; there, also, the meals are taken in Summer time. Alongside of numerous pieces of furniture and implements installed here, a large collection of Engadine buck-sledges **The buck-** strikes the eye. **sledges**

To many a visitor particular interest may attach to the big iron bear's-trap, the services of which the grand- **The bear's trap** father of the founder of the Museum well knew how to appreciate.

Room II
Dwelling-
room in an
Engadine pea-
sant's home
from Zuoz;
middle of XVII
century

To the left of the Entrance-gate, a low door leads up a few steps into the dwelling-room, which, with its ceiling inside-faced beam-wainscoting, its cupboard in carved work on the one side, and on the other side of the door the stove, shows the very type of an Engadine "stube" (parlour). Opposite the stove the table is placed, and along the walls run simple wooden benches. Behind the stove with its quaint wooden lattice-work, a narrow door opens on a narrow stairs, the "Burel". Through a small opening in the ceiling this stove-stairs leads up into the chamber above.

Room III
The kitchen

Back of this "stube" (dwelling-room), in accordance with the typical arrangement of the various rooms in the Engadine peasant's home, is the Kitchen (Cha da fö or Cuschina). It opens on the Suler by an iron door. The furnishing of this somewhat gloomy, vaulted place is rather

The fire-place scanty. Along one of the two longer walls the fire-place is installed, on top of a projecting low stone-wall, that supports is. It is called "Platta", shortly. Above it, there are seen hanging on long chains and moveable iron-bars, the bronze-cooking-pots, while a gigantic chimney-funnel in the shape of a pyramid "chappa da chamin" gathers in the smoke, drawing it on into the open air. All kinds of kitchen-utensils ornament the wide base of this pyramidal chimney. Alongside of the hearth there lies towards the outer wall of the house the fire-ditch (Foura). Above this open fire-place, there hangs the milk-kettle (chaldera) from a horizontal iron-bar fitted like an arm into a vertical beam, that may be set to describe a semi-circle. In a niche in the wall opposite, there is standing the big copper water-kettle. In another niche, beyond the kitchen-door, behind a wooden lattice-door the milk-pots are kept. All sorts of furniture, tools and utensils, such as the daily needs of a household half peasantry and half "burgher" may suggest, fill up the rest of the room.

The idea of setting up the characteristic oven in the shape of a hemisphere, and projecting to the outside of the house-wall, resting on some beams, had, we are sorry to say, to be relinquished.

Stairs of stone under a vaulted ceiling lead us up to the first story. From the Suler it is shut off by a low wooden lattice-gate, so that no fowl nor any other small domestic animal may undertake to pay visits in the dwelling rooms above.

Stairs to the I. story

The room in the first story nearest to the stairs was taken from Brail in the Lower-Engadine. Its walls are of timber set in yokes. The beams of the ceiling are irregularly studded with round Medaillons, themselves ornamented on their outlines with indentations. An inscription carved in the wall advises us of the fact, that the house, in which this one room once was the dwelling-room, had been erected in the year 1580; its owner and skilful architect are named at the same time. Notice the plain-carvings on the furniture and the queer stove-frame. The considerable number of spinning-wheels and similar appliances recall the times when, on long evenings in winter-time, girls and women of a neighbourhood would meet with their wheels and distaffs to spin in company (saira da filadè) and listen to the charming or awful stories and fairy-tales, as the case might be, that grand-mother could tell from near the stove.

Room IV
From a house in Brail, Lower-Engadine; dated 1580

Spinning-room

A low door opens on a real Engadine baroc-room from about 1670. It is the so-called upper or better-room (stube) from the very same house as the room on the ground-floor The stove shows a little more of artistic treatment than those others in the rooms already described. A tower-like super-structure with coloured profiles crowns it; on the contrary, its frame is of a simpler type.

Room V
Best room, the so-called "stüva sur" from an Engadine peasant's-house in Zuoz, middle or end of XVII century

Along a small corridor, where several pieces of furniture have found room, we reach the state-room of the family of the à Marca's in Mesocco. An inscription on the ceiling again recalls the name of the builder, the skilful cabinet-maker, to whose artistic taste we owe this room. It dates from 1621. The wainscoting as well as the furn-

Room VI
Small corridor

State-room from the house of the à Marca family in Mesocco, Date 1621

iture from the Mesocco go to prove, that at that time a native art of ornamentation had struck root and developed in that valley beyond the Alps, and that possibly this one artist had been its founder or chief representative. This particular original ornamentation is mainly characterised by an additional development of its elements which in themselves appear simple, but now give the impression of richness by means of small scales added to those simpler forms, the scales thus producing the same effect as do our wooden scaly linings on the outside of houses. Small ornamental rose-diamonds are punched on these scales as well as on the underlying material. Particularly rich appears the lid of the strong-box, on which 25 different rosettes set one-another off. The door-frame, cupboard and table have always belonged to this room; the picturesque stove, however, comes from the valley of Bregaglia. It is built on the Winterthur-type and shows the same kind of green Relief-tiles with the somewhat frivolous allegory of the five senses, as do the beautiful stoves in the residences of the Nobles at Wülflingen and Elgg.

Room VIII Antichambre, imitation of a vaulted hall in Scanfs, middle of XVII century

On the way back along this same short corridor, we enter a vaulted antichambre in Stucco. This hall suggests a seigniorial residence, of which it once formed part, such as are not unfrequently met with in the Engadine. Old weapons and furniture decorate it. Small iron doors remind us of the good old custom of our fore-fathers, to heat the stoves of the dwelling-rooms from the out-side. A double-folded door leads to a covered balcony, spacious and of stone, from which the eye roams over the lake and the whole watering-place. This door admits the visitor directly to the first floor.

Room IX State-room of the house of the Visconti-Venosta in Grosio (Valtellina); beginning of the XVII century

By a larger door we enter the State-room of the house of the Visconti-Venosta in Grosio, Valtellina, which valley, for centuries, had been a domain subject to and misruled by the Republic of the three Leagues of the Grisons (down to the Peace of Campo Formio, 1797, on which occasion

Napoleon I. dictated the terms to Austria and the Grisons at the same time). It is supposed, that at one time it served the purpose of a Hall of Justice, and tradition has it, that it was the scene, where the leaders of the Catholics of the valley plotted the murder of all the Protestants of yon country. Certain it is, that it dates from the beginning of the XVII. century. The ornaments are in rich Italian Baroc style; on the ceiling they encircle and set off three magnificent coats of arms. The walls are horizontally divided into two fields; the lower one is covered with wainscoting, the upper edge of which carries a fine cornice. Graceful Karyatides support it instead of pillars, their lower extremeties ending in long bodies of the shape of fishes, curiously entwined. The upper part of the bodies represent men and women of every stage of life, some of them with a great deal of expression in their carved heads. Whether or not these pensive, weeping or despairing creatures in company with men of dignified appearence really had borne any relation to the use, to which this apartment was put as a Hall of Justice, is not altogether clear and certain, but it is probable that they did have. Correspondingly, the narrow stripe of the upper wainscoting shows little child's figures standing. The stove of green Relief tiles together with the frame belongs to this room, the wooden parts of which are of the native Arve-tree and still exhale to this day the sharp yet pleasant scent.

On the second floor we reach first a spacious corridor **Second floor.** with plenty of light; close to its wooden ceiling, on the **Room X** walls painted in white, a broad frieze of sgraffito-painting **Corridors** attracts the eye. It is copied from the original in a Plantahouse at Samaden, dating from the year 1589 and representing, in roughly drawn curves, phantastically assembled, some fabulous creatures on which children ride, naked. Their procession is interrupted now and then by the coats of arms of a number of families of local prominence in this country. The artist who is responsible for these freaks, may have belonged to that class of masters who kept wandering working for a living. Apparently he had nothing to complain of the fare and cheer in that Planta-house; and the uncouthness of some of the lines of his drawings might well be traced back to the good Veltliner wine. Here, again, many objects of furniture in the native styles have found a place. A sliding-window of characteristic construction is seen here; it, by the way, affords a splendid view of the lake.

Room XI Engadine sitting-room of the XVIII century

Through a door, on the left hand of this corridor, we enter an Engadine sitting-room, of the 18th century. In somewhat stiff and bare forms the wooden ceiling imitates the Stucco-work of that period and correspondingly simple is also the wainscoting. Perhaps it is just this simplicity which awakens in us the pleasant sensation, that is distinctly felt in this room, and which is by no means diminished or paralized by the fact, that the furniture is in the style Louis XVI, and, with its finely polished greaves, forms a striking contrast to the pine-wood wainscoting in its natural colour. On the other hand, this contrast proves, how little our ancestors used to make of "style" and how naively they would put in their rooms any piece of furniture, provided it suited its purpose. The furniture comes from Süs and bears the coat of arms of the Bonorands.

Collection of prints and manuscripts in Romane Language

A collection of prints and manuscripts is likewise placed here.

Room XII Neo-gothic Sleeping-room from Präsanz (Oberhalbstein)

Bed with tester from the time of the plague

Adjacent to this "Stube" (parlour), suiting it as a sleeping-room, as it were, one enters a smaller room in neo-gothic style; it is taken from Präsanz and dates from 1570/80 or thereabouts. The closet, chest and bed with a tester, on which latter a large gruesome skeleton keeps grinning down, is all there is in the way of furniture in this little room. Possibly, the painting belongs to one of those dreadful periods during which the plague hunted mankind as far up as these high Alpine valleys, otherwise of so healthy a climate, and made such deep impression on their minds that they could not cease to think of death and constantly kept its spectre before their eyes.

On the opposite side of the corridor there is likewise a sitting-room in neo-gothic style from Savognino. It resembles the one preceding very closely. It is fitted up as a public-house such as were, without great changes, to be found for centuries in the inns on all international highways across the Alps in the Grison-country. In excellent keeping with the rest of this interior a stove in green tiles is found here, which really comes from a guest's room in Bergün, a community that was by law under the obligation to open by day and by night the door of yon room to any wanderer coming along. If it could speak, how much would this old companion be in a position to tell of the events, to which it was a witness itself, and of the people, who would confide one-another their doings and happenings, hopes and fears, while warming their frozen limbs in its hospitable neighbourhood. That it is an old stove, is clearly to be seen from the armoured horsemen on some of the tiles showing the fashion of the middle of the 15th century. The same applies to the heraldic use of the capricorn or wild goat of Coire, so much in favour and appearing only a few decades later.

Room XIII Neo-gothic room from Savognino (valley of Oberhalbstein) **Date 1579**

Guest's room of an inn

Close by this guest's room, we find the Chamineda (store-room). Its floor is paved with cobble stones, its coolness quite noticeable. Here stands assembled a complete assortment of house-furniture such as the particular needs of the inhabitants of an Alpine valley have evolved in the course of centuries.

Room XIV Chamineda Store-room

From the first landing on the stairs to the garret we turn to a small chamber containing a selection of rare minerals and stuffed native animals, such as a Grison Nobleman, who generally was also a bold hunter and naturalist, used to establish and maintain and show to his guests when telling them of his exploits and adventures of

Room XV Museum of Natural History

the chase. This collection replaced for him the Art-galleries of the Patricians of the cities.

Here also are exhibited the interesting collection of Alpine plants of the late teacher Mr. Fluor of Muot Marias-Sils, as well as those other collections of the same kind and interest, namely, the one of Zernez and the other of the Buffalora, kindly put, as a deposit, at the disposition of the Engadine Museum by Dr. Bezzola, Esq. in Ermatingen.

Room XVI Exhibition room:

In a more spacious hall near by, old paintings and portraits, mostly of Italian origine, are on show.

Paintings (Single paintings are for sale)

A choice collection of bed-steads and cradles shew the evolution of the native technics and styles in that line; besides, alongside, a smaller collection of chests with entailed work is worthy of notice; the same may be said of a number of old musical instruments.

Room XVII Corridor in the garret

In the garret a roomy corridor receives us. Here some more furniture together with closets full of the picturesque Engadine costumes and tissues! Not alone the number, but also the quality of the work here shown bespeak a high degree of proficiency in embroidery and lace-work; for which occupations the inhabitants, in consequence of the climatic conditions under which they had to live, tethered down month for month to their four walls, as they were, must have had ample time. Notice yet, in this room, an inscription on a beam in the ceiling. The beam comes from the house of the Jenatsch's in Samaden.

Room XVIII Gothic hall from the building of the stewardship of the episcopal domain in Savognino

Through a door, flanked by two others, we enter a room in high gothic Style from the house of the stewards in Savognino managing for the bishop of Coire. It may date yet further back than 1500, and its rich decorative work would indicate the abode of a man of quality. Gothic chests and tables of manifold constructions make up a contemporary inventory, whereas the cupboard, for want of one in gothic style, belongs to a later period. It bears the date 1663, and comes from the present poor-house of Obervaz. The names of its first owners are recalled by the coat of arms of the families of the v. Vaz and Bergamin. A wooden tablet with a painted Saint, hanging by the door, is not to be overlooked.

In the basement of the house there is, in place of the so-called Cuort (court) of the Engadine-house, an exposition of duplicates of all kinds, which eventually are for Sale.

Regulation of visits
to the Engadine Museum.

I. Time of visits.

The Museum is open:

On Week-days from $9^1/_2$ to 12 o'clock
   and ,, 3 ,, 6 ,,
On Sundays ,, 9 ,, 12 ,,

II. Conditions of visiting.

Entrance money: On Week-days frcs. 2.—
       ,, Sundays ,, 1.—
Subscription for 1906 . . . . ,, 10.—

Children under 6 years may not visit at all; children under 13 years only in company with adults.

Schools accompanied by their teachers get cheap rates.

III. Miscellaneous remarks.

1) Smoking within the Museum is prohibited.
2) Dogs must not be taken to the Museum.
3) To persons *either drunk* or *unmannerly* admission to, or stay in the Museum will be refused.

CPSIA information can be obtained
at www.ICGtesting.com
Printed in the USA
LVOW10s0029220218

567415LV00055B/878/P